FLOCK OF BIRDS AF
FOR BUILDING A BOOK
RECOMMENDATION SYSTEM

Dr. Akshi Kumar
Dept. of Computer Science & Engineering
Delhi Technological University

Contents

Abstract

With the advent of Web 2.0 also known as Social web, user is actively participating in contributing to the content of a particular platform that means that one can get to know enough about a particular user i.e. his taste in various domains such as clothing, movies, music, books, food, places etc so that he can be suggested with new genre of various things which he may like but this process of recommendations on basis of activities performed by a particular user often faces a barrier that is known as Information Overload.

This problem is solved by using information filtering tools that are widely known as recommender systems. More formally, recommender Systems are the platforms that make personalized recommendations for a particular user by predicting the ratings for various items. Any recommender system is based upon either the information/features provided about a particular object or similarity between two users or items. Feature selection has a significant role in recognizing these features and improving the recommendation accuracy. Owing to the high- dimensional datasets, this problem of recommendation manifolds, thus fostering the need to look for improved & optimized techniques for feature selection.

Swarm Intelligence is an emerging area in evolutionary computing that makes use of different naturally occurring phenomena followed in different aspects of life, particularly by different agents. Since these phenomena have been evolved over a lot of years, they provide a way to find optimal solutions to problems by following a heuristic. The work presented in this book puts forward a swarm intelligence based book recommender system built on the collaborative behavior of bird flocks using category information about books. The standard Book-Crossings dataset has been used to evaluate the research study. This technique combines the ability of the flock of birds' algorithm to form clusters of similar users with the algorithm to find similar books to generate recommendations. It is capable of removing many challenges that are faced while generating recommendations.

The book is organized into 4 chapters. Chapter 1 briefly describes the recommender systems, its techniques and prominent challenges which motivate this research work. Chapter 2 expounds the proposed model, the book recommendation system using flock of birds algorithm. Chapter 3 describes the experiments carried and results obtained on the Book-Crossing dataset. Finally, chapter 4 summarizes the conclusion drawn from experimental results and presents some possible future directions.

Acknowledgements

I am most thankful to my parents for constantly encouraging me and giving extensive support in my academic activities. I am extremely grateful to MPS Bhatia, Professor, Netaji Subhas Institute of Technology, Delhi, India for being a constant source of inspiration throughout my research and teaching career. Special thanks to my bestie and my son for being my strength throughout.

I also take this opportunity to thank my undergraduate scholars Rochak and Anshu in the Department of Computer Science & Engineering, Delhi Technological University, Delhi, India for working with me on the work presented in this book.

List of Figures

Chapter 1

Recommender Systems

In the last decade, there has been a massive growth in the amount of data and information available to us. Every day, more books and journals are published, more newspaper articles are written, more web pages are generated, more office documents are stacked, more photos are taken, and more movies are produced, reviewed and rated. With such a large amount of data, it becomes more and more difficult to get information one truly desires. Here, Recommender Systems come into play. They build a knowledge graph, which over the time is improved, to find the information best suitable for you.

A lot of research has been done in Recommender Systems. From how the data is wrangled to how it is used for generating proper recommendations, a lot of new techniques have been developed. Some of these techniques as taken from [1] are -

- Content-based / Item-based: In this filtering approach, we recommend items to the user that are similar to the ones the user has liked in the past or are similar to the user profile in attributes. It is a very common technique. In this, a number of attributes are determined for books and users using which we generate a weighted result in which items that are recommender first are the ones that suit the similarity criteria the best.
- Collaborative: In this approach, we use information about the past ratings of users, to generate a similarity measure between each user. This similarity measure is then used to generate recommendations for the user using the nearby

similar users. This concept is what that gives this technique the name *Collaborative Filtering*, because it is the collaborative nature of users that drives the ability to find similar items.

- Knowledge Engineering / Rule-based: This technique is the one that is most used right now. In this, the user answers several questions, until receiving a customized result such as a list of products. A problem with this technique is the proper formulation of questions that can actually contribute to some information extraction from the user. These questions tend to be about the attributes that define different rules so that they can be used to define some rules for the user.

- Demographic: In demographic recommender systems, items are recommended to users based on their demographic attributes, such as gender, age, location, etc. The recommendations can be based on stereotypes derived from different machine learning techniques or marketing, that learn to predict users' preferences from their demographic attributes. For example, users can be classified into groups based on their attributes, and this information can then be used for generating recommendations.

- Hybrid: This technique is just a combination of two or more already defined techniques to use the best features of each. It is what we are doing in this work. We are using content information about items to determine similar items and collaborative behavior to form clusters of users, to generate a smaller domain to work with.

A clustering problem can be defined as - *given a set of n data points in a visualization plane, partition them into k clusters such that data points in each cluster possess some common characteristic or state.* Numerous clustering algorithms exist in such context [2]. A very well-known algorithm is the k-means algorithm [3] which takes an input parameter, k, and partitions a set of n objects into k clusters so that the resulting intra-cluster similarity is high but the inter-cluster similarity is low.

Many of the modern clustering algorithms and recommender systems use bio-inspired principles. Such a swarm-intelligence algorithm, *Flock of Birds* [4], has been used. One major advantage of such algorithms is that they work in a distributed way often capable of finding the global solution rather than getting stuck in local optima. Furthermore, they do not require any prerequisites such as initial partitioning of users or items and thus they are good for clustering data. It can be defined as - *a number of points in a visualization plane in which each point moves towards another similar point in such way that after some iterations similar points seem to move together in groups.* The inspiration is the birds flying in the sky in flocks, with direction of each bird towards the direction of the overall flock.

Reynolds [5] proposes an approach to build a simulation of the flock using a boid model that supports geometric flight and then add behaviors that correspond to the opposing forces of collision avoidance and the urge to join the flock. Defined rules by Sak and Olfa [1] in order of decreasing precedence, the behaviors that lead to simulated flocking are -

- Collision Avoidance - avoid collisions with nearby flockmates
- Velocity Matching - attempt to match of a boid velocity with its nearby/close flockmates.
- Flock Centring - attempt to stay close to nearby flockmates.

Velocity is a vector, a combination of direction and speed. Similarly, the meaning nearby in these rules is a key to the flocking process. One boid's awareness on another is based on the distance and direction of the speed vector between them.

Static *collision avoidance* and dynamic *velocity matching* are complementary. Together they ensure that the members of a flock are free to fly within the crowded skies of the flock's interior without running into one another. Collision avoidance is the urge to steer away from an imminent impact. Static collision avoidance is based on the relative position of the flockmates and ignores their velocity. Conversely, velocity matching is based only on velocity and ignores position. With velocity matching, separations between boids remain *approximately invariant* with respect to on-going geometric flight. Static collision avoidance serves to establish the minimum required separation distance; velocity matching tends to maintain it.

Flock centring is a process inwhich a boid want to be near the centre of the flock which reflects the centre of the nearby boids. Flock centering causes the boid to fly in a direction that moves it closer to the centroid of the nearby boids. If a boid is present deep inside a flock, the population density in its neighborhood is roughly the same thus the boid density is also approximately the same in all directions. In this case, the flock centering urge is small because the centroid of the neighborhood boids is approximately at the centre of the neighborhood. But if a boid is on the boundary of the flock, its neighboring boids are on one side. The centroid of the neighborhood boids is displaced from the centre of the neighborhood toward the body of the flock. Here the flock centering urge is stronger and the flight path will be deflected somewhat toward the local flock centre.

Since we are building a recommender system for books, we have chosen the *Book-Crossing dataset* for our work. This work is thus a representation of how the content information of items can be successfully used with the collaborative information about users to develop a recommendation engine that can scale to a big database with information continuously flowing in. Thus, it can be used for different datasets by modifying it differently for each, to extract the content information of items. Typically, with Recommendation Systems, we face the following problems as given in [6] -

- Sparsity Problem: It directly affects the quality of recommendation and thus is one of the major problems encountered in recommender systems. The main reason behind data sparsity is that most users do not intend to rate most of the items or are lazy to rate items and thus the available ratings data is usually sparse. Collaborative filtering suffers from this problem because it is dependent over the user-item rating matrix in most cases.

- Cold Start Problem: It refers to the situation when a new user or item just enters the system. There are three kinds of cold start problems - new user problem, new item problem and the new system problem. In the case of a new user, very less information is already available that can be used to generate recommendations. In case of a new item, no ratings are available for it from other users. Thus collaborative filtering fails. However, content based filtering can provide recommendation in case of a new item as it does not rely on any previous rating information of other users to generate recommendations.

- Scalability: Scalability is the property of the system that indicates its ability to handle growing amount of information in a graceful manner. With the amount of information available over the internet skyrocketing with time, it is obvious that the recommender systems are having an explosion of data and thus need to handle it. As the number of users and items grow, computation and complexity of recommender system also increases. In collaborative filtering, computations grow exponentially and get expensive, sometimes leading to inaccurate results. Methods are proposed to deal with it using approximation techniques. However, most of the time they result in accuracy reduction.

- Over Specialization Problem: When users are restricted to getting recommendations resembling already known it is termed as over specialization. It prevents user from discovering new items and other available options. Diversity of recommendations is a desirable feature of all recommendation system.

The proposed approach intends to solve most of these problems. It provides a generalized approach wherein the various cases encountered during recommendation are analyzed and treated with the recommendation procedure best suited for it. A lot of research has been done in improving efficiency of recommender systems to give better recommendations to the user with the aim to improve results. Various clustering and optimization techniques have also been used for this purpose [7].

Genetic Algorithms have been applied to the clustering problem using several different encodings. For example, artificial ants based algorithms have modeled the way insects can organize objects into groups according to their similarity. One can observe a similar nature in flocks of birds. They can have spectacular and complex shapes. These shapes serve various goals like avoiding predators, saving energy (like in the case of the flight of ducks).

(a)   (b)

Figure 1.1: A visualization of the system in which the flock of birds moves [4]. Starting from the initial positions

(a) where birds are randomly placed (with random direction), we wish to obtain the final situation

(b) where similar birds move in a coherent way (in the same direction and close to each other).

The model presented in this work is based on placing birds (data points) in a 2d visualization space using the same simple decision rules that are used in flocks: get close to similar points; get away from dissimilar points. These rules are such that, after a given number of iterations, groups of homogeneous points are created (see Figure 3.1). Work has already been done on this, but not extensively. Moreover, it does not take into account much of the problems that concern the recommender systems. Our model solves these problems by providing the best procedure for generating recommendations depending upon what user we are catering to and what book we are trying to recommend.

Chapter 2

The Proposed Model

2.1. The System Architecture

The following figure 2.1 illustrates the basic architecture of the proposed system.

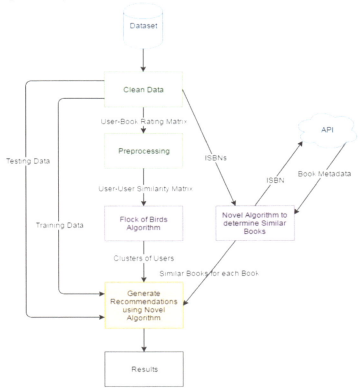

Figure 2.1: The System Architecture

The architectural flow can be understood in the following steps -

1. We are using the Book-Crossing dataset as input. It includes information about the users, the books and what rating, if available, a user has given to a book.
2. We analyze the dataset using different queries and extract whatever information we need to continue with our process. We then split this data into Training and Testing data.
3. Training data is used to perform the clustering of users on the basis of the Flock of Birds algorithm.
4. The ISBNdb book API is used to extract the category information about the books. This information includes a list of categories to which the book belongs. The category is represented in the form of a hierarchy. Using our novel approach, we find, for each book, books similar to it.
5. After obtaining the cluster of users and the similar books for each book, we proceed with generating recommendations.
6. The performance of the algorithm is then tested on the Testing data. It is then compared with already available recommendation approaches.

In the next section, we present the details of the Flock of Birds algorithm.

2.2. Flock of Birds Algorithm

Flocking behavior can be described as the behavior exhibited when a group of birds, called a flock, are foraging or in flight. Birds adjust their physical movement to avoid predators, seek food and mates, optimize environmental parameters such as temperature, etc. Birds have poor eyesight and they move in flocks in order to identify the obstacles in their paths. Essentially the basic models of flocking behavior are controlled by three simple rules: 1. Separation - avoid crowding neighbors (short range repulsion) 2. Alignment - steer towards average heading of neighbors 3. Cohesion - steer towards average position of neighbors (long range attraction). This section presents view to the core clustering algorithm given by Picarougne [4].

Consider a set of n data (or examples) denoted by $(e_1, ...e_n)$ that one wishes to cluster. These data can be encoded with any kind of representation language as long as there exist a similarity function among the data. For two data e_i and e_j, this function is denoted by Sim(i, j), and has values in $[0, 1]$. A value 1 means that two data are extremely similar.

---

1) **Read** the n data $(e_1, ...e_n)$.
2) **Place** (randomly for instance) the n agents in the 2D environment.
3) **while** iteration <MaxIteration**do**
   a) Compute a new position for each of the n agents according to the same local rule.
   b) Move (simultaneously) all agents.
4) **endwhile**
5) **Build** (possibly) clusters from the flock of agents and Output them.

Figure 2.2: The main algorithm for controlling agents.

Consider a population of n agents where the ith agent represents data e_i. Agents move in a 2D environment, as represented in figure 1.1.

An agent i is characterized by its real coordinates $(x_i, y_i) \in [0, 1] \times [0, 1]$ and by its speed vector $v_i = A_i \hat{v}_i$. Here, A_i $(A_i \geq 0)$ denotes the amplitude of the speed vector and $\hat{v}_i$ $(||\hat{v}_i|| = 1)$ its normalized direction. The 2D Euclidean distance between two agents i and j is denoted by $d(i, j)$. The main algorithm for controlling agents (Figure 4.1) works as follows - initially, all agents are placed at uniform random positions and are given a uniform random initial speed. The ideal distances are then computed for each couple of agents. Then, agents will move and decide, according to a local rule, whether they must get closer to each other or not, and whether they should go in the same direction or not. Intuitively, this rule has two goals - to establish an ideal distance between agents that is representative of the similarities of the data they represent, and to let agents with similar data move in the same direction. From this local rule, groups of agents that move together will emerge (see Figure 2.2): these groups define a partitioning of the data set.

The computation of agent is done as follows:

---

1) Compute i's neighborhood:
$$V(i) = \{j \mid j \in [1, n], j \neq i, d(i, j) \leq d_{th}\}$$

2) Compute a new direction $\hat{v}_i(t + 1)$:

3) if $V(i) = \phi$ then

$$\hat{v}_i(t + 1) \leftarrow \hat{v}_i(t)$$

4) else
for each agent $j \in V(i)$ do

if $d(i, j) > d^*(i, j)$ then
$$\beta(i, j) \leftarrow 4 \times \left(\frac{d(i,j) - d^*(i,j)}{d_{th} - d^*(i,j)}\right)^2 \quad /* \text{ attraction } */$$

---

end if

if $d(i, j) = d^*(i, j)$ then

$$\beta(i, j) \leftarrow 0$$

end if

if $d(i, j) < d^*(i, j)$ then

$$\beta(i, j) \leftarrow -4 \times \left(1 - \frac{d(i,j)}{d^*(i,j)}\right)^2 \quad /* \text{ rejection } */$$

end if

The influence of j over i is then:

$$v_{\text{resulting}}(i, j) \leftarrow \hat{v}_j(t) + \beta(i,j) \times \hat{v}_{ij}(t)$$

end for

Compute the sum of influences:

$$w(i) \leftarrow \Sigma_{j \in V(i)} \quad v_{\text{resulting}}(i, j)$$

New direction : $\hat{v}_i(t + 1) \leftarrow \frac{w(i)}{||w(i)||}$ considering that

the angle between $\hat{v}_i(t + 1)$ and $\hat{v}_i(t)$ is limited to

90 degrees.

5) **end if**
6) Compute a new amplitude :

$$A_i(t + 1) = A_{i_{def}} + \left(\frac{d_{th}}{20 \times (|V(i)| + 1)}\right)$$

7) Compute the move for agent i (all agents are moved at the same time):

$$(x_i(t + 1), y_i(t + 1)) = (x_i(t), y_i(t)) + A_i(t + 1) \hat{v}_i(t + 1)$$

Figure 2.3: Computing the move of agent i.

2.2.1. Explanation

Figure 2.3 shows how the movement of all the agents that changes with each iteration. For every agent, this algorithm [4] calculates a new direction and amplitude based on its previous values and also, on the values of its neighboring agents. For agent i, the neighborhood $V(i)$ is the set of all agents j located at a distance $d(i, j)$ that is less or equal than d_{th}, where d_{th} is the threshold below which an agent will be able to perceive another agent (set to 0.05 experiment purposes), and below which the two agents can influence each other. The distance $d(i, j)$ is the Euclidean distance between two agents i and j at every iteration of loop is calculated via Equation (1) -

$$d(i,j) = ||\widehat{e}_i - \widehat{e}_j|| \tag{1}$$

Then two situations arise - if there is no agent in $i's$ neighborhood, then i will keep moving in the same direction $\widehat{v}_i$ with an amplitude A_i set to d_{min}. When $i's$ neighborhood contains one or more agents, the influence of those agents over i can be described as - the change of speed vector direction, on one hand, and the change of speed vector amplitude, on the other.

The *ideal distance* $d^*(i, j)$ is computed via Equation (2), where $Sim(i, j)$ is the similarity between two users i and j *and* Sim_{th} is the similarity threshold. If this similarity $Sim(i, j)$ is small and if the two users are too close to each other, then they should move away from each other.

$$d^*(i,j) = \left(\frac{1 - Sim(i,j)}{1 - Sim_{th}(i,j)} \right) \times d_{th} \tag{2}$$

According to Equation (2) :-

1. If Sim(i, j) is equal to the threshold Sim_{th}, then the two agents should be placed exactly at the limit of their neighborhood ($d^*(i, j) = d_{th}$).
2. If Sim(i, j) $<\text{Sim}_{th}$, then the movement should try to separate these two neighbors.
3. If Sim(i, j) $>\text{Sim}_{th}$, then the two agents should stay in their neighborhood at a given distance ($d^*(i, j) <d_{th}$).

Sim_{th} can be computed according to the following formula in *equation (3)* :-

$$\text{Sim}_{th} = \frac{1}{2} (\text{Sim}_{average} + \text{Sim}_{max}) \qquad (3)$$

Where $\text{Sim}_{average}$ and Sim_{max} are the respective mean and maximum similarity between the n users.

Every iteration of the loop in Figure 4, $v_{resulting}(i, j)$, the influence of j over i in terms of direction, depends on the distance $d(i, j)$ with respect to an ideal distance $d^*(i, j)$ and on the angle between the speed vectors of j and i (respectively denoted by $\hat{v}_j$ and $\hat{v}_i$) shown in Equation (4).

$$v_{resulting}(i, j) = \hat{v}_j(t) + \beta(i, j) \times \hat{v}_{ij}(t) \qquad (4)$$

This vector $v_{resulting}(i, j)$ has two components: one will tend to align the movements of both agents i and j and the other one represents an attraction or rejection between both agents as follows :-

1. If the distance between the two users is greater than the ideal distance
   ($d(i, j) >d^*(i, j)$), then an attraction takes place between the two agents.
2. If $d(i, j) = d^*(i, j)$, then the speed vector of i simply becomes aligned to that of j, while staying at the ideal distance.

3. If $d(i, j) < d^*(i, j)$, then a rejection between i and j takes place because they are too close to one another.

$\beta(i, j)$ takes positive, zero , or negative values according to these three cases previously enumerated (Figure 2.4). Then finally, $w(i)$ represents the new desired direction for user i, provided that they are limited in the change of direction they can perform, in order to produce realistic displacements.

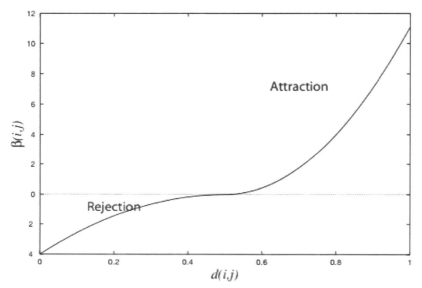

Figure 2.4: $\beta(i, j)$ as a function of the distance d(i, j)

The speed vector of agent i is computed using the formula mentioned at line 6 in the algorithm in figure 2.3. The first component determines the agent's minimum speed, i.e., the A_{idef} parameter which has been experimentally set to $\frac{1}{5}d_{th}$. This

value of A_{idef} ensures that no user will stand alone and still in the visualization plane without the possibility of meeting other users and no user will move fast enough to become directly placed in the centre of a group.

If any dissimilar user would get into the centre of group that will dismantle the group and thus any user will only be continuously attracted or rejected by a group. Users travelling alone will always have greater speed than user travelling alone which is ensured by second component of A_{idef} parameter.

Isolated users will keep on hopping from one to group to another until they find a group that accepts them. The time is considered discrete and at each t, all users move synchronously and update their position and speed at every time step. To keep all the users inbound a technique called *Phasing* is used. According to that a boundary of the visualization space is treated as an entry point to its opposite boundary, i.e, when any user reaches the boundary of the space, it phases into it and makes a comeback from its directly opposite boundary with all other parameters same as before.

2.2.2. Stopping Criterion

In order to define the convergence of our algorithm, we have used the same simple criterion that measures the spatial disorder of users as specified in [4]. The 2D visualization space ($[0, 1] \times [0, 1]$) is divided onto a 2D matrix of size 5×5.

The size of the matrix has been adjusted through experiments in order to have a better tradeoff between the precision of the computation of the 2D disorder and the computational cost of this computation. The number of users that are located now in each cell (i, j) is calculated and stored into $p(i, j)$. The spatial entropy is defined as the disorder or the randomness of the system (inspired from Shannon's definition [8]) in Equation (5):

$$ES(t) = -\sum_{i=1}^{5}\sum_{j=1}^{5} p(i,j)\,\ln p(i,j) \qquad (5)$$

The stopping criterion for our iterations is based on the entropy measure described in Equation (5) and is - if the observed minimum entropy has not been improved since the last 100, 200 and 300 iterations, then the algorithm stops. These thresholds have been experimentally determined.

2.3. Content Based Algorithm

This section illustrates the content-based algorithm for book recommendation system.

---

for each book i **do**

  $S \leftarrow []$ *// A list of books similar to i*
  Sort i's categorical hierarchies alphabetically.
  Split i's categorical hierarchies by '.' so that each can now be represented as a list of nodes.
  Sort i's categorical hierarchies on the basis of their length in the decreasing order (length refers to the number of nodes one has to traverse in the category tree to reach the corresponding category).

  $L \leftarrow$ categorical hierarchies   *// A list*

  $V \leftarrow \{\}$ *// A set representing books already visited*

  $Priority \leftarrow 1$ *// Priority of the book being encountered*
  while L is not empty **do**

    $new\_L \leftarrow []$ *// A new list which will be assigned to L in the future*
    for each categorical hierarchy c in L **do**
      for each book j in the c **do**

```
                        If j ∉ V then
                            Add j to V
                            Append pair (j,Priority) to S
                    end if
                end for
                ifc has more than one node then
                    Remove last node from c
                    Append c to new_L
                end if
            end for

            L ← new_L
            Priority ← Priority + 1
        end while
end for
```

Figure 2.5: The main algorithm for finding similar books

Figure 2.5 shows how the books similar to each book are obtained. Here, each book belongs to one or more categorical hierarchies. For each book, we first define the list S that will store the books similar to it, along with their priorities in the form of a tuple. We then sort the list containing categorical hierarchies alphabetically. We then split each categorical hierarchy in this list by '.' so that it can be represented as a list of nodes to be traversed while going through the category tree. This list is then sorted on the basis of the number of nodes in the categorical hierarchy in the descending order. This list is then assigned to L which denotes the categorical hierarchies yet to be traversed. A set V is defined which maintains the books that have already been appended to S. *Priority* is initialized to 1. Here, a low value of *Priority* indicates a higher similarity.

Then we start a loop which keeps on running until L becomes empty. Inside this loop, we define a new list new_L. This list signifies the new categorical hierarchies that will be worked with in the next iteration of the while loop. Then, for each categorical hierarchy, we find the books belonging to it using a recursive function.

The recursive function traverses down the category tree till it reaches the last node. After reaching the last node, it returns all the books belonging to that node, as well as all the ones that belong to any category branching from that node. Why this is done will be elaborated further. For each book found in the categorical hierarchy being considered, we check if it was already appended to S or not. This information is maintained by V as mentioned above. Thus, if the book is present in V, it is discarded. Otherwise, it is appended to S along with its priority. After this, we check if the categorical hierarchy has more than one node or not. If it doesn't, it is discarded. Otherwise, its last node is removed and it is then added to new_L. After every categorical hierarchy has been traversed, new_Lassigned to L and *Priority* is increased by 1.

The reason for sorting the list alphabetically, splitting it on '.' and then sorting it on the basis of the number of nodes in the categorical hierarchy forms the core of our algorithm. It is inspired from the simple idea that the greater the number of nodes in the categorical hierarchy, more we have to traverse the category tree and as such more specialized is the category. This ensures that we find books in specialized category first before proceeding towards the generalized ones. This is also the reason why we are removing the last node from each categorical hierarchy before appending it to new_L. By removing the last node, we, in the next iteration will look for similar books belonging to the same categorical hierarchy but less specialized. This is the reason why we are decreasing the priority of the similar books obtained with every iteration of the outermost while loop.

Chapter 3

Experimentation and Results

Book-Crossing dataset - http://www2.informatik.uni-freiburg.de/~cziegler/BX/ - isdataset we have used in our work. This dataset contains 278,858 users providing 1,149,780 ratings about 271,379 books. It is extremely sparse. To deal with the sparsity, we wrote a lot of queries to analyse it. Essentially, we decided to work with users belong to the United States because they were the ones who were responsible for most of the ratings. We, then took the top 250 most rated books by those users, and the top 100 most rating users. This brought down the sparsity by a 3000. We randomize these books and split them into training and testing as 50% and 50%. We set d_{th} to 0.05 (determined experimentally), maximum number of iterations to 1000 and minimum number of users in a cluster to 3, and ran the prediction procedures for Collaborative Filtering with Flock of Birds on training and testing books and HybridBookRecom on training, testing as well as testing from training books for 10 times averaging the results. This process is repeated for different number of threshold steps - 100, 200. The prediction procedures for different techniques are –

3.1. General Prediction Procedure for CF + F Algorithm

$U \leftarrow$ Set of all users

$B \leftarrow$ Set of all books

$A \leftarrow |U| \times |B|$ matrix - actual ratings of $|U|$ users for $|B|$ books

$P \leftarrow |U| \times |B|$ matrix - predicted ratings of $|U|$ users for $|B|$ books - initially 0

$S\_u \leftarrow |U| \times |U|$ matrix - user similarity matrix

for each cluster c **do**

    for each user i in c **do**

        for each book j in B **do**

            if $A[i][j] > 0$ **then**

            Sort users in cluster c in decreasing order of their similarity to i

            $s \leftarrow 0$

            for each user k in cluster c **do**

                if $k \neq i$ **and** $A[k][j] > 0$ **then**

                $P[i][j] \leftarrow P[i][j]$ +

                $A[k][j] \times S\_u[i][k]$

                $s \leftarrow s + S\_u[i][k]$

                end if

            end for

```
                    end for
                    if c has more than one node then
                            Remove last node from c
                            Append c to new_L
                    end if
            end for
            L ← new_L
            Priority ← Priority + 1
        end while
end for
```

Figure 3.1: Procedure for Collaborative Filtering + Flock of Birds

The above algorithm is pretty trivial. It is a standard Collaborative Filtering approach where instead of using all the users as neighbors, only the users present in the same cluster obtained from Flock of Birds algorithm are used. Even so, to calculate the predicted rating for a particular book for a particular user, we take a weighted average of ratings for that same book given by all the users classified as neighbors. If no such ratings are found, the prediction is set to be the same as the actual to ensure that it doesn't contribute to the error and accuracy calculations.

3.2. General Prediction Procedure for HBR Algorithm

The above algorithm is quite different from the one given in Figure 3.1. Here, we also utilize the books similar to the book for which rating is to be predicted. This information is stored in S_b. First, we check if the book for which rating is to be predicted has similar books or not.

If it doesn't, we take a weighted average of ratings for that same book given by all the users classified as neighbors to the current user (these neighbors are the users present in the same cluster as the given user obtained using Flock of Birds Algorithm). If it does, we define a submatrix of the order $max\_u \times max\_b$. This submatrix represents the top

max_uneighbors of all the neighbors and the top max_btrainingbooks of all the training books thatwe will be using to predict the rating for the book under consideration. If no ratings are found in this matrix, the prediction is set to be the same as the actual to ensure that it doesn't contribute to the error and accuracy calculations. If ratings are present, we, instead of using just a weighted average by user-user-similarity, also use the book-book-similarity measure calculated using priority such that its value is inversely proportional to the priority, to represent a true priority. First we subtract the priority of the book from 11, and then divide the result by 10, thus lesser the value of priority, higher the similarity.

$U \leftarrow$ Set of all users

$B \leftarrow$ Set of all training books

$A \leftarrow |U| \times |B|$ matrix - actual ratings of $|U|$ users for $|B|$ books

$P \leftarrow |U| \times |B|$ matrix - predicted ratings of $|U|$ users for $|B|$ books - initially 0

$S\_u \leftarrow |U| \times |U|$ matrix - user similarity matrix

$S\_b \leftarrow$ list of $|B|$ *sets* - each set represents books similar to a book in B

for each cluster c **do**

    for each user i in c **do**

        for each book j in B **do**

            if $A[i][j] > 0$ **then**

                Sort users in cluster c in decreasing order of their similarity to i

                $s \leftarrow 0$

                if $S\_b[j]$ is empty **then**

                    for each user k in cluster c **do**

                        if $k \neq i$ **and** $A[k][j] > 0$ **then**

                        $P[i][j] \leftarrow P[i][j] + A[k][j] \times S\_u[i][k]$

                        $s \leftarrow s + S\_u[i][k]$

                      end if

                    end for

                else

                    $max\_b \leftarrow 3$

                    $b \leftarrow 0$

for each book l in $S\_b[j]$ **do**
$max\_u \leftarrow 3$

$u \leftarrow 0$

for each user k in cluster c**do**
if$k \neq i$ **and**$A[k][j] > 0$ **then**

$$P[i][j] \leftarrow P[i][j] + A[k][j] \times S\_u[i][k] \times \frac{11 - Priority(l)}{10}$$

$s \leftarrow s$ +

$S\_u[i][k]$
$\times$
$\frac{11 - Priority(l)}{10}$

end if
$u \leftarrow u + 1$

if$u = max\_u$**then**
break
end if
end for
$b \leftarrow b + 1$

if$b = max\_b$**then**
break
end if

end for
end if
if$s > 0$ **then**
$$P[i][j] \leftarrow \frac{P[i][j]}{s}$$

else
$$P[i][j] \leftarrow A[i][j]$$

end if
end if

```
                     end for
          end for
  end for
```

Figure 3.2: The general prediction procedure for HybridBookRecom

3.3. Prediction Procedure for new books using HBR Algorithm

```
U←Set of all users

B_train←Set of all training books

B_test←Set of all testing books

A ← |U| × |B_train| matrix - actual ratings of |U| users for

|B_train| books
P ← |U| × |B_test| matrix - predicted ratings of |U| users

for |B_test| books - initially 0
S_u← |U| × |U| matrix - user similarity matrix

S_b←list of |B_test| sets - each set represents books similar

toabook in B_test
for each cluster cdo
        foreach user i in c do
                for each book j in B_testdo
                        ifA[i][j] > 0 then
                                Sort users in cluster c in
                                decreasing order of their
                                similarity to i
                                s←0
```

If S_b[j]is empty **then**

    for each book l in B_train**do**

        if$A[i][l]$ > 0 **then**

        $P[i][j] \leftarrow P[i][j] + A[i][l]$

        $s \leftarrow s + 1$

        end if

    end for

else

    $max\_b \leftarrow 3$

    $b \leftarrow 0$

    for each book l in S_b[j] **do**

        $max\_u \leftarrow 3$

        $u \leftarrow 0$

        for each user k in cluster c**do**

        if$k \neq i$ **and**$A[k][j] > 0$ **then**

$$P[i][j] \leftarrow P[i][j] + A[k][j] \times S\_u[i][k] \times \frac{11 - Priority(l)}{10}$$

        $s \leftarrow s$

        $S\_u[i][k]$

        $\times$

        $\frac{11 - Priority(l)}{10}$

        end if

        $u \leftarrow u + 1$

        if$u = max\_u$**then**

        break

        end if

        end for

```
                                    b ← b + 1

                                    if b = max_b then
                                    break
                                    end if
                                    end for
                                    end if
                                    if s > 0 then
```
$$P[i][j] \leftarrow \frac{P[i][j]}{s}$$

```
                                    else
```
$$P[i][j] \leftarrow A[i][j]$$

```
                        end if
                    end if
                end for
            end for
        end for
```

Figure 3.3: The prediction procedure for new books using HybridBookRecom

The above algorithm is very much similar to the one given in Figure 3.2. One change is that it introduces two different sets of B, B_train and B_test. These signify that this algorithm is used for the prediction of new books, B_test, using information from the past books, B_train. Also we have changed that the case in which the book for which rating is to be predicted has no similar books. In this , we just take an average of the ratings given by the user being considered for all the training books. The reason for doing this is simple. We don't have a particular set of books on which we can define our sub matrix. As such, we resort to using the only information that is available to us.

As for evaluation, we have calculated 4 different criteria - Mean Absolute Error (MAE), Root Mean Square Error (RMSE), Accuracy and Mean Average Precision(MAP). Accuracy is subjected to the constraint that a rating of ±2 error

was considered to be the same as the actual. MAP is subjected to the constraint the books that were given rating greater than 5 belong to the relevant set. The results obtained for MAE, RMSE and Accuracy show that our algorithm consistently outperforms the Collaborative Filtering with Flock of Birds. The only case where it falls behind is when it comes to recommending books that are ranked - in MAP.

3.4. Analysis

The results when threshold steps are set to 100:

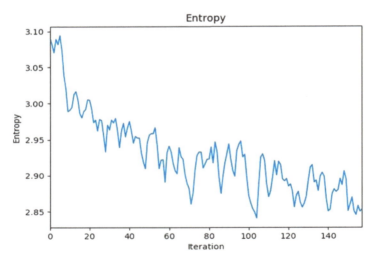

Figure 3.4: Entropy vs Iteration for threshold steps = 100

- *Running CF + F and HBR to predict training books -*

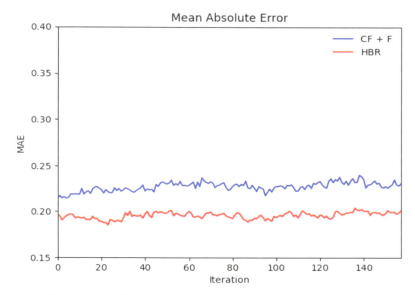

Figure 3.5: Training - MAE vs Iteration for threshold steps = 100

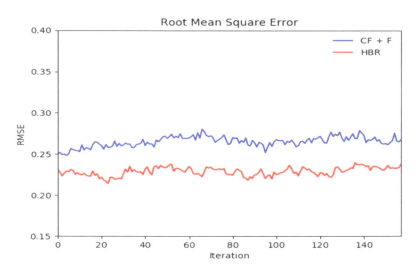

Figure 3.6: Training - RMSE vs Iteration for threshold steps = 100

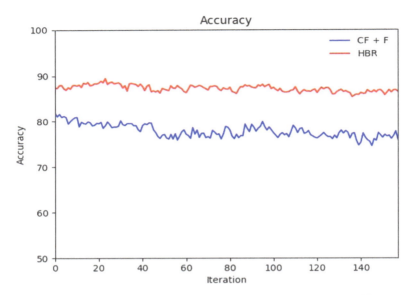

Figure 3.7: Training - Accuracy vs Iteration for threshold steps = 100

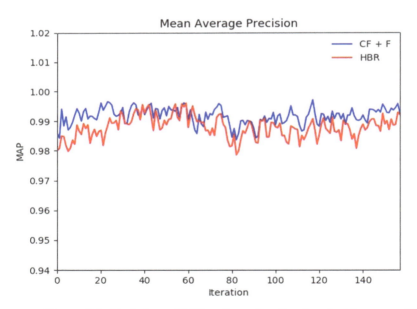

Figure 3.8: Training - MAP vs Iteration for threshold steps = 100

- *Running CF + F and HBR to predict testing*

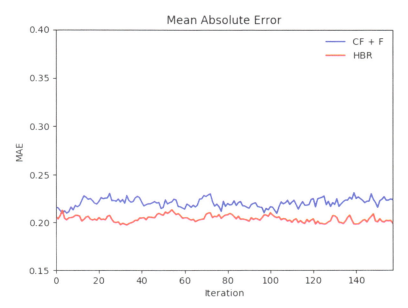

Figure 3.9: Testing - MAE vs Iteration for threshold steps = 100

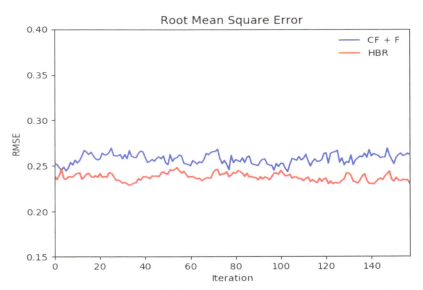

Figure 3.10: Testing - RMSE vs Iteration for threshold steps = 100

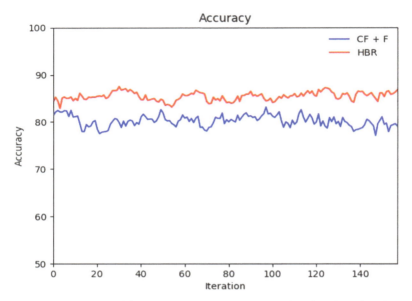

Figure 3.11: Testing - Accuracy vs Iteration for threshold steps = 100

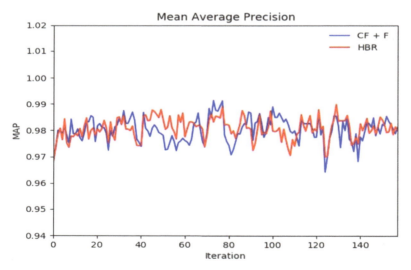

Figure 3.12: Testing - MAP vs Iteration for threshold steps = 100

- *Running HBR for predicting testing books using training books -*

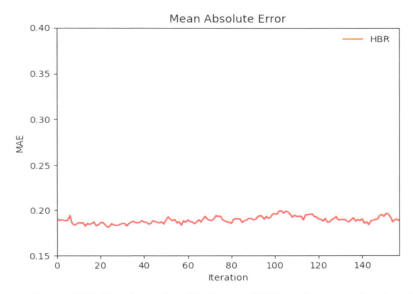

Figure 3.13: Testing using Training - MAE vs Iteration for threshold steps = 100

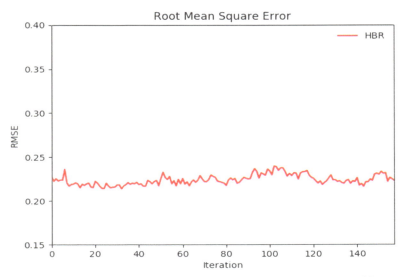

Figure 3.14: Testing using Training - RMSE vs Iteration for threshold steps = 100

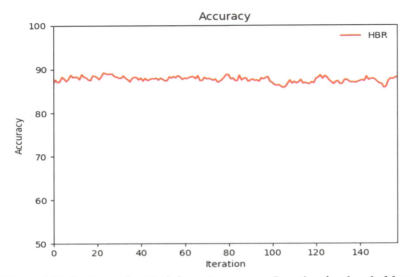

Figure 3.15: Testing using Training - Accuracy vs Iteration for threshold steps = 100

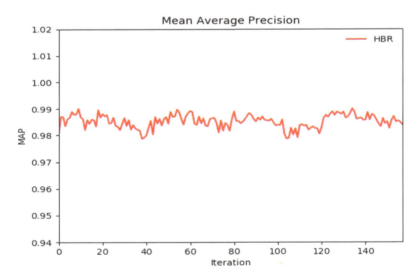

Figure 3.16: Testing using Training - MAP vs Iteration for threshold steps = 100

The results when threshold steps are set to 200 -

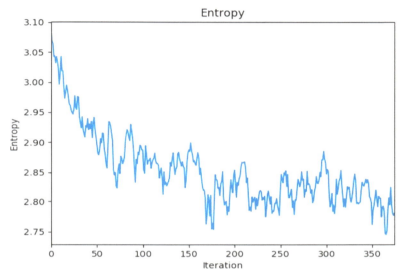

Figure 3.17: Entropy vs Iteration for threshold steps = 200

- *Running CF + F and HBR to predict training books -*

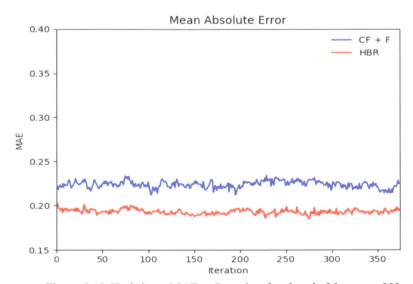

Figure 3.18: Training - MAE vs Iteration for threshold steps = 200

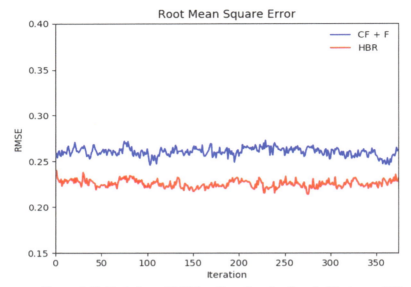

Figure 3.19: Training - RMSE vs Iteration for threshold steps = 200

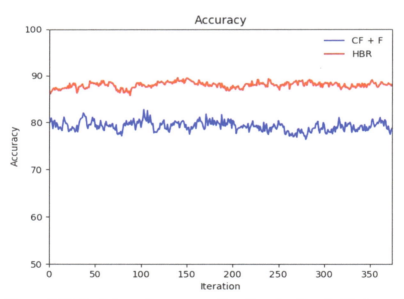

Figure 3.20: Training - Accuracy vs Iteration for threshold steps = 200

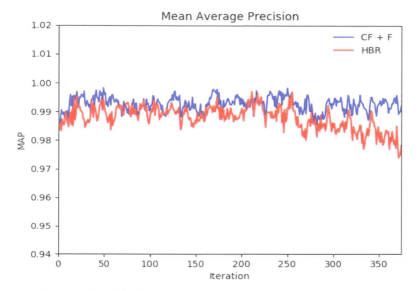

Figure 3.21: Training - MAP vs Iteration for threshold steps = 200

- *Running CF + F and HBR to predict testing books -*

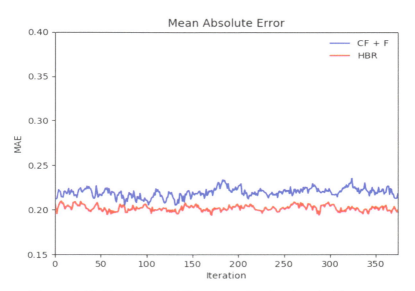

Figure 3.22: Testing - MAE vs Iteration for threshold steps = 200

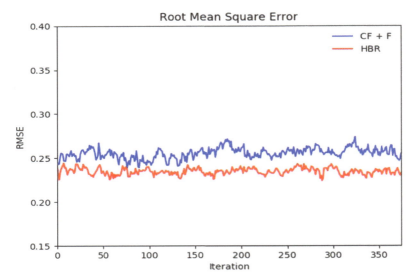

Figure 3.23: Testing - RMSE vs Iteration for threshold steps = 200

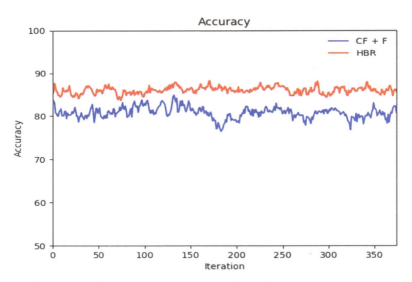

Figure 3.24: Testing - Accuracy vs Iteration for threshold steps = 200

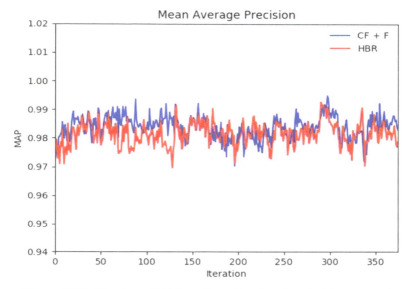

Figure 3.25: Testing - MAP vs Iteration for threshold steps = 200

- *Running HBR for predicting testing books using training books -*

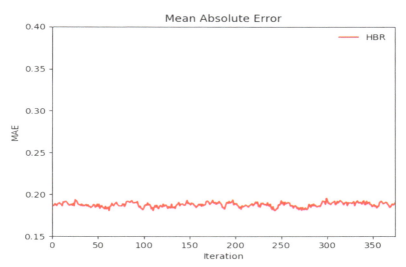

Figure 3.26: Testing using Training - MAE vs Iteration for threshold steps = 200

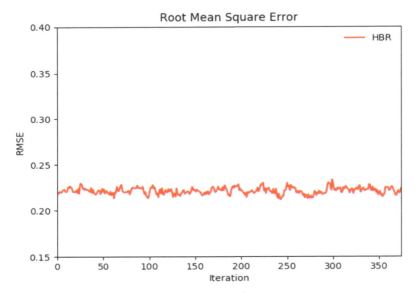

Figure 3.27: Testing using Training - RMSE vs Iteration for threshold steps = 200

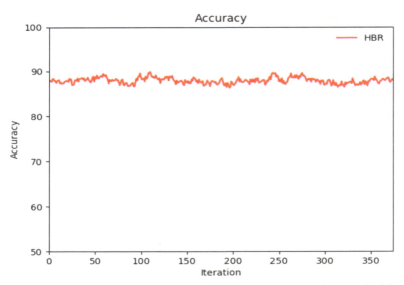

Figure 3.28: Testing using Training - Accuracy vs Iteration for threshold steps = 200

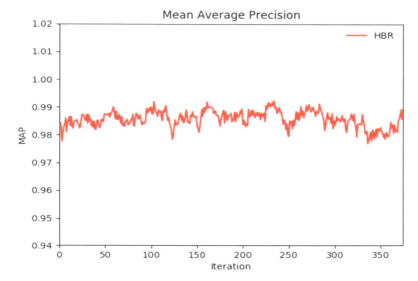

Figure 3.29: Testing using Training - MAP vs Iteration for threshold
steps = 200

Chapter 4

Conclusion and Future work

In this work we have described a new approach that combines a content based approach, used to find similar books for every book, with a swarm intelligence algorithm - Flock of Birds, used to obtain clusters of similar users. Clusters generated from Flock of Birds help in ascertaining a lot of information like the number of clusters formed, their shapes, the similarity of the data they contain and effect of noisy data. Categorical hierarchies help to find books similar to every book. This knowledge helps us in recommending new books that come into the system. Also, if we need to build a distributed recommender system, books can be recommended to new users on the basis of their demographics and thus helps in improving the scalability of the system. This approach also works well with sparse datasets. Thus, our model helps in solving most of the problems encountered while generating recommendations.

There are a certain limitations to our model. As of now, it fails to improve upon the already existing model in terms of recommending a ranked list of books. Thus, work can be done to extend our model so that this limitation can be overcome. Also, we have defined this model to work for recommending books.

We can try applying this approach to other datasets as well. We can try extending it to use it in distributed recommender systems to generate recommendations for new users by using demographics. We can work on improving the algorithm used to find books similar to a book. We can use algorithms that can help tune the manually set parameters to their optimal values depending upon different characteristics of the dataset. A number of algorithms are available in that domain. The information that can be obtained from data is a key to improving the already existing recommender systems. To find a way that can better extract the data, deal with its inconsistencies and manipulate it to suit our requirements is a challenge of its own that we wish to embark on.

References

1. Saka, Esin, and OlfaNasraoui. "A recommender system based on the collaborative behavior of bird flocks." *Collaborative Computing: Networking, Applications and Worksharing (CollaborateCom), 2010 6th International Conference on.* IEEE, 2010.
2. Jain, Anil K., and Richard C. Dubes. *Algorithms for clustering data.* Prentice-Hall, Inc., 1988.
3. MacQueen, James. "Some methods for classification and analysis of multivariate observations." *Proceedings of the fifth Berkeley symposium on mathematical statistics and probability.* Vol. 1. No. 14. 1967.
4. Picarougne, Fabien, et al. "A new approach of data clustering using a flock of agents." *Evolutionary Computation* 15.3 (2007): 345-367.
5. Reynolds, Craig W. "Flocks, herds and schools: A distributed behavioral model." *ACM SIGGRAPH computer graphics* 21.4 (1987): 25-34.
6. Sharma, Lalita, and Anju Gera. "A survey of recommendation system: Research challenges." *International Journal of Engineering Trends and Technology (IJETT)* 4.5 (2013): 1989-1992.
7. Kumar, Akshi, Khorwal, Renu and Chaudhary Shweta. "A Survey on Sentiment Analysis using Swarm Intelligence." *Indian Journal of Science and Technology* 9.39 (2016).
8. Shannon, C. E. "A mathematical theory of communication, bell System technical Journal 27: 379-423 and 623–656." *Mathematical Reviews (MathSciNet): MR10, 133e* (1948).
9. Ziegler, Cai-Nicolas, et al. "Improving recommendation lists through topic diversification." *Proceedings of the 14th international conference on World Wide Web.* ACM, 2005.
10. Kumar, Akshi, Pulkit Tanwar, and Saurabh Nigam. "Survey and evaluation of food recommendation systems and techniques." *Computing for Sustainable Global Development (INDIACom), 2016 3rd International Conference on.* IEEE, 2016.